OH SWEET MINNIE

LINDA ESTES

Energion Publications
Gonzalez, Florida
2023

Copyright © 2023, Linda Estes. All Rights Reserved

Scripture quotations taken from the New American Standard Bible® (NASB), Copyright © 1960, 1962, 1963, 1968, 1971, 1972, 1973, 1975, 1977, 1995 by The Lockman Foundation. Used by permission. www.Lockman.org

Cover Image: Linda Estes
Cover Design: Henry Neufeld

ISBN: 978-1-63199-877-5
eISBN: 978-1-63199-878-2

Energion Publications
P. O. Box 841
Gonzalez, Florida 32560

pubs@energion.com
energion.com

TABLE OF CONTENTS

In the Beginning 1
All Things Great and Small 5
What a Thief! 9
Do You See What I See? 12
Who Is Training Who? 15
Loving Care 18
What Would You Pay? 22
What a Treasure! 25
How Close Can You Get? 28
And the Battle Is On 31
Location, Location, Location 34
Hide and Seek 37
Hair, Hair and More Hair 40
To Be or Not To Be … Content That Is??!! 43
Routine or Bust 46
Do I Get a Treat for That? 49
Patience, Patience, and More Patience 52
And Before We Close … 55

IN THE BEGINNING

Every story has a beginning and I pray this story of how I became Minnie's mom blesses you as much as our story blessed me. The Morkie on the cover of this book is my sweet Minnie. When I first heard that Minnie was a Morkie, I had to look that bred up to see what I was getting. I found out that Morkies are part Maltese and part Yorkie. My vet and I think Minnie is more Yorkie than Maltese. She was eight months old when I took the cover picture of her and she is now just over a year old. She brings me so much joy, and she continues to be good for my mind, body and soul. If you have or have ever had a furry friend, I am sure you understand that sentiment.

When I decided I wanted to get a little dog, I was experiencing bouts of loneliness. Being a widow and living alone, my house was just too quiet for me. The silence was often deafening, and I knew I needed more life in my home. The Lord and I talked about this a lot and when I felt peace about it, the search began to find the perfect puppy for my needs. I spent months filling out applications and searching at shelters and online for a puppy I could rescue. My applications were rejected time and time again for some of the craziest reasons, or at least I thought they were crazy. Did I have another dog? No…application rejected. Was I going to let the dog sleep with me? No…application rejected. Was I planning on working outside the home? Yes…application rejected. But then, I found a breeder online that was selling her miniature Schnauzer in a nearby state. She and I corresponded back and forth, and I made plans to buy her dog. The night before

I was to pick her up, I felt a strong urge to ask the owner for another picture of Maggie (yes, I already named her) so I could see what she looked like after her grooming. The owner sent me a picture and my heart dropped to my feet. You see, I had told her that I needed a dog that weighed ten pounds or less and she assured me that Maggie fit that requirement, but that picture showed a different story. I took that picture and showed my sister, brother-in-law and niece in hopes that they would see things differently than I had. We all agreed that Maggie was at least 25 if not 30 pounds. Again, my heart sank. Why would someone lie about that? Didn't she know that a picture is worth a thousand words? Needless to say, I didn't buy her.

That was pretty much my last straw on my dog search. I told God that I was done searching for the right dog. I was emotionally spent! God and I had talked about me getting a dog and I was certain that I had been given the green light to do just that but now I was tired of all the rejections, lies and the endless applications that I had been filling out for months. My heart couldn't take another rejection, and I told God that if He wanted me to have a dog, He was going to have to drop one in my lap. And I know now that was all God was waiting for me to do…take my hands off the situation and let Him work things out in my life.

My family and friends knew what had been happening with the dog search and how broken-hearted I was thinking I had found the dog I longed for, just to have it be another dead end. But then things changed. One of my friends posted on a social media site that she had a friend (I was that friend) who was a widow and a heart patient who was looking for a dog weighing less than ten pounds. The next day she got a response to her post. That was Sunday morning, just two days after I was supposed to pick up Maggie. My friend corresponded with the lady who had this puppy and told her that she was going to see me at church in a few minutes and that I would call her as soon as church

was over. My friend couldn't wait to tell me the news at church and I have to say that I had a hard time listening to my pastor's message that morning. My thoughts just kept coming back to this Morkie that needed a new home. Was this the one God was dropping in my lap? My thoughts raced for the next hour or so. As soon as church was over, I called the owner's daughter and after an extremely sweet conversation, we both agreed that their Morkie was going to be perfect for me. We made plans for me to pick up the puppy after work on Monday, and as the saying goes, the rest is history.

On Monday, as had been arranged, my sister and I went to pick up the puppy. We met with the owner's daughter and quickly learned why we weren't picking up the puppy from the actual owner, her dad. Her dad's name was Kirk and sadly, he was in the hospital. My heart ached for Kirk after I heard his story. His daughter told us that Kirk worked from home and on the day of the accident, he was in the kitchen getting a cup of coffee when everything changed for him. His neighbor was cleaning his gun at the same time Kirk was getting coffee. Unfortunately, the neighbor didn't check the chamber of his gun before he started cleaning it. As a result, the gun discharged, and the bullet came shooting through Kirk's kitchen and struck Kirk below the waist. It was so tragic and so needless! Not only because he was shot but now he couldn't take care of his four-month-old puppy. I couldn't imagine how hard of a decision it was for him to say that his sweet puppy needed a new home. Thankfully Kirk survived his accident, but his recovery was going to take a long time and he just couldn't care for his little Morkie. As crazy as it is, life often has a way of dictating some of our decisions and this was one of those times. Winnie, as Kirk called her, became Minnie the day I picked her up. Minnie was so much easier for us to pronounce, and the name fit her perfectly as she only weighed about five pounds. Now she weighs just over seven pounds and Minnie's vet said that he doesn't expect her to get much bigger

than she is now, which is a perfect size for me to handle. She is loved and spoiled by all that see her. Minnie has been my sweet companion for about ten months, and I am amazed at all the lessons God has shown me through her. Throughout this book, you will be reading about some of those lessons and the way God has blessed me through having Minnie in my life. Who knew that I could learn and be reminded of so many of God's truths from a little, seven-pound Morkie!

> Dear Heavenly Father, thank you for speaking to us in so many ways. Your Word tells us in Romans 1:20 that You speak to us through everything You have created. You have not hidden Yourself from any of us. Over the past months, You have spoken volumes to me through Minnie. My prayer for this book is that You will speak to all that read it so their eyes and heart can be opened to You. I pray these things in Your Son's precious name. Amen.

ALL THINGS GREAT AND SMALL

James 1:17 tells us that "every good and perfect gift is from above, coming down from the Father of the heavenly lights, who does not change like shifting shadows." Sometimes people only see the good things that God provides when it is something big, like healing someone from cancer or allowing them to buy a house. Those are indeed good gifts from God but over the course of our days, there are as many, if not more, small blessings as there are large blessings. We might just have to look harder to recognize them, but once you start looking, I know you will be amazed at all the small blessings God showers upon you throughout your day.

In case you are questioning whether that statement is true, I have a challenge for you. Pick one day of the week to test this statement. Journal all the blessings you can see from the time you wake up until the time you go to bed. Keep a notepad with you or use your phone to make a list of the blessings. The first blessing on your list should be that you woke up and were given another day to serve the Lord here on earth. And no matter what kind of day you have, the last item on your list should be that God helped you get through this day and that now He will give you rest. If we really focus on everything as a blessing from God above, I imagine you will have dozens upon dozens of blessings over the course of your day to write down.

Minnie was one of those blessings from above! I told you the story of how I got her and it was easy to see God's hand all over the situation that brought me to adopt Minnie. When I got her, she still needed to finish out her puppy shots, so I used the same veterinarian as the previous owner had used. The first time I took her to that vet's office, I received confirmation that Minnie was a gift from God. During my discussion with the vet, I was told that Minnie's birthday was August 1. To that news, my eyes filled with tears. For you see, that was the same birthday as my late husband, Alan. Once the vet heard that information, she wrote on Minnie's chart, "Minnie, a blessing from heaven," to which I totally agreed!

Many know the story in the Bible about how God fed the 5,000+ people with just five loaves of bread and two fish. This story can be found in Matthew 14:13-21, Mark 6:30-44, Luke 9:10-17, and in John 6:1-15. In this story, God showed the disciples that anything was possible with God. It might have seemed like a small blessing to those receiving the food, but to the disciples who knew that God only started out with a meager amount of food, it was a huge blessing! Thousands of people witnessed this miracle from God. But there might be a story in the Bible that you might be less familiar with. This Old Testament story is found in 1 Kings 17:8-16. The story where God speaks instructions to Elijah reads as follows:

> Then the word of the LORD came to him, saying, 'Arise, go to Zarephath, which belongs to Sidon, and stay there; behold, I have commanded a widow there to provide food for you.' So he arose and went to Zarephath, and when he came to the entrance of the city, behold, a widow was there gathering sticks; and he called to her and said, 'Please get me a little water in a cup, so that I may drink.' As she was going to get it, he called to her and said, 'Please bring me a piece of bread in your hand.' But she said, 'As the LORD your God lives, I have no food, only a handful of flour in the

bowl and a little oil in the jar; and behold, I am gathering a few sticks so that I may go in and prepare it for me and my son, so that we may eat it and die.' However, Elijah said to her, 'Do not fear; go, do as you have said. Just make me a little bread loaf from it first and bring it out to me, and afterward you may make one for yourself and your son. For this is what the LORD, the God of Israel says: 'The bowl of flour shall not be used up, nor shall the jar of oil become empty, until the day that the LORD provides rain on the face of the earth.' So she went and did everything in accordance with the word of Elijah, and she and he and her household ate for many days. The bowl of flour was not used up, nor did the jar of oil become empty, in accordance with the work of the LORD which He spoke through Elijah.

This story did not impact 5,000+ people, like the story of the five loaves of bread and two fish did, but it had a great impact on Elijah, the widow and her son. So, what about your life? Are you looking to fill a basic need like having enough food to eat, or needing to fill a lonely part of your life? Have you talked to the Lord about your needs? He already knows what you are needing, but He might be waiting, like in my case, for you to take your hands off the situation and let Him work things out as only He can. We serve a God who not only knows every need we have in our life, even before we ever ask, but has a way to provide for everything we need. My prayer for you is that you would let God show you that He cares about every detail of your life, both big and small, and that He is able to handle anything that touches your life. May you tuck the truth of Psalm 55:22 in your heart. "Cast your burden upon the Lord and He will sustain you; He will never allow the righteous to be shaken."

Dear Heavenly Father, we praise You for Your compassion and love. You know everything we need even before we even ask. May we give all our worries, cares, and difficulties to You. Help us to take our hands off our needs and give them to You, so You can give us exactly what we need, exactly when we need it. We ask these things in Your Son's precious name. Amen.

WHAT A THIEF!

One of the things that Minnie's previous owner told me was that she loves socks. Not only does she love socks and loves to steal and hide them, she loves all kinds of paper products. Napkins, paper towels, tissues, toilet paper and even receipts in your purse. She also loves stealing my mail and pulling things out of the trash cans. So, during the first month that I had Minnie, I had to "Minnie proof" my home. All bathroom doors stay closed to avoid a stream of toilet paper being pulled through the house. Trash cans now have lids on them, and tissue boxes are now positioned out of her reach. I have a table next to the chair I sit in a lot and everything on the table had to be put in baskets to keep her from stealing whatever is there. Minnie only measures about a foot in height, but she has an amazing vertical jump. And she is so fast that you don't see her stealing things until she's heading back to the ground with the item in her mouth.

I removed everything from the floor that I didn't want her to get into except the iRobot floor vacuum because it needed to stay plugged in and it must remain on the floor to do its job. She used to mess with it all the time, but I fixed that. I can turn on this floor vacuum from my phone. Minnie was having a day where she just wasn't listening to anything I had to say so I thought a lesson on "what was hers and what wasn't hers" was in order. I waited until she started messing with the iRobot, and then using my phone, I turned the floor vacuum on. It came flying off its charging base right at Minnie which totally spooked that little puppy. That's all it took for Minnie to learn to leave

it alone. That lesson gave me quite a chuckle as Minnie jumped into my lap for safety.

Although Minnie is quite the thief, she really does little harm. It's mostly just cute and her thievery has become a game. But there is one thief whose work is quite serious and there is nothing funny about what he does. I'm referring to Satan. John 10:10 tells us why Satan is here. "The thief comes only to steal, and kill, and destroy." He is here to steal everything he can from us. His line of destruction started from the beginning. Genesis 3:1-6 lays out the first sin, or deception, of mankind. In the Garden of Eden, the serpent, Satan, convinced Eve that if she ate from the "tree of life" in which God instructed her not to eat from or even touch, that she wouldn't die like God said she would. The enemy fed her a big, fat lie in Genesis 3:5 when he told her, "For God knows that in the day you eat from it your eyes will be opened, and you will be like God, knowing good and evil." And just like Satan does today, he presents a twisted version of the truth, one that tempts us to go against what God has to say. He constantly tries to steal people away from God. He tries to deceive us like he did with Adam and Eve.

We are told in John 8:44 that Satan is the father of lies. His thievery started in Genesis with Adam and Eve and continues through Revelation. Throughout all of time, he tries to deceive people, thus stealing them away from God. Revelation 12:9 tells us that there is coming a day when Satan's days of deceit will come to an end. "And the great dragon was thrown down, the serpent of old who is called the devil and Satan, who deceives the whole world; he was thrown down to the earth, and his angels were thrown down with him." Even though we know that at the end of time, Satan will be destroyed, we need to be aware of his deceit in our day-to-day life. 1 Peter 5:8 tells us to "Be of sober spirit, be on the alert. Your adversary, the devil, prowls about like a roaring lion, seeking someone to devour." The best way to be on the alert is to spend time in God's word. Without knowing

what God has to say, we won't know if we are being deceived by Satan. One thing we must remember about Satan is that even though he can leave a trail of destruction in our lives, God has him on a leash. Just like when I take Minnie outside on a leash, she can only go as far as the leash will allow. God is sovereign over Satan. He can do no more than what God says he can do.

Even though Satan knows he is on a leash, he tries his best to make us stumble. As I told you already, Minnie is all about speed. Satan uses that tactic, too. He tries to get us to do something or make a decision quickly, so we don't have time to talk to God about it. So for me, that's a huge red flag! If I'm told I need to make a fast decision so I won't miss out, my answer will be "no." By doing that, and not acting under pressure, the only thing I miss out on is regret later on. That's one game Satan always loses with me. Have you figured out some of the tactics he uses with you?

It's true that sometimes Satan wins small battles in our life by stealing those things that God provides for us. Things like His forgiveness and His peace. But when we realize that we have strayed away from what God has for us, we can always run back to Him and jump in His lap, just like Minnie did when she learned that some things are not meant for her.

> Dear Heavenly Father, thank You for the truths that You provide for us in Your Word. Thank You for telling us that Satan is on the prowl looking for someone he can devour and that You have given us in Your Word the tools we need to combat Satan's attacks. And when we find that we have strayed from You, thank You for being merciful and for extending Your grace to us when we ask for Your forgiveness. And thank You that we know You are sovereign and that Satan will not win. The victory is Yours! Please help us stand strong against the things of the enemy. And it is in Your Son's precious name we pray. Amen.

DO YOU SEE WHAT I SEE?

"Do you see what I see?" If I asked Minnie that question, she would have to say, "No, I don't see what you see." And I would have to agree with her answer. You see, Minnie is only a foot tall from the top of her head to the bottom of her feet. Her visual perspective is much different from mine just because she sits so close to the ground. In order for her to see most things, she has to look up. The only time that she has a better vantage point is when she jumps up to sit in my lap. When she does that, she jumps in my lap and then stands up on her back legs which allows her to put her front legs on my chest and her nose on my nose. It's almost as if she is saying, "Now I can see what you see!" It always makes me laugh when she's looking eye to eye with me.

Our visual perspective should be like Minnie's. As believers in Jesus Christ, we need to be "looking up" to see things as God sees them. 1 Chronicles 16:11 tells us to, "Seek the LORD and His strength; seek His face continually." Those exact words are also found in Psalm 105:4. I love it when scripture is this clear. So, how is God's perspective different from what ours is? Well, God's perspective is an eternal perspective. Seeing things through God's eyes can have a great impact on every aspect of our life.

We live in a fallen world and sin runs rampant. Without a relationship with our heavenly Father, we could easily get discouraged and even lose hope. The only place we can find security is in our relationship with God. As we seek Him, we learn to see things as He sees them. Take sin for example. Once we accept Jesus Christ as our Lord and Savior, our old sinful life is replaced

as we are a new creation in Him. The enemy would love for us to believe that there are sins that God just won't forgive but scripture clearly tells us that is not true. Psalm 103:12 says that God has removed our sins as far as the east is from the west. And Jeremiah 31:34 tells us He will forgive our sins and will remember them no more. As believers in Jesus Christ, we are forgiven. We are a new creation. And we are a precious child of God. Looking at life with this perspective, God's perspective, changes everything!

Does being forgiven and being a new creation in Jesus Christ mean that we will never have storms blow through our life? No, we will still have challenges in life, but seeing those challenges from God's perspective will allow us to go through those trials with total confidence that there is nothing that the enemy can do to cause us to lose our eternal security that we have in Jesus Christ. Romans 8:38-39 confirms this statement. "For I am convinced that neither death, nor life, nor angels, nor principalities, nor things present, nor things to come, no powers, nor height, nor depth, nor any other created thing, will be able to separate us from the love of God, which is in Christ Jesus our Lord."

As we continue to seek the Lord, He will show us how to live a life that will be pleasing to Him. He will guide and direct us as to how we need to be a witness of His great love. The enemy will do everything he can to make us think that our sins will keep us from being used by God for His kingdom. Looking back through scripture shows us that once again the enemy is lying when he tries to convince us of that. Some of the great Old Testament saints dealt with sins in their lives. Abraham, who was known as the father of faith, at one point feared for his life. He lied and asked his wife to lie, by telling Pharaoh and others that his wife was actually his sister. But God still used him to further His kingdom. Moses did not follow God's orders completely and thus was kept from entering the Promised Land. But God still used him to bring God's people out of Egypt and used him to

bring us the Ten Commandments. King David, who God called a man after His own heart, committed adultery and murder but God still used him mightily to grow the Kingdom of God.

You see, God knows we are not perfect, but He still accepts us and will use us in spite of our sins. The enemy will try to convince you otherwise, but we need to remember that Satan is known as the father of lies. He doesn't want us to look at our life through God's perspective. He wants us to think that if we sin, and we are all going to sin, that God will cast us out and won't love us anymore. The truth from God is that when we accept the gift of salvation through Jesus Christ, all of our sins – past, present and future – are totally forgiven. And anything the enemy says contrary to that just proves that he is a liar. Seeing things from God's perspective, instead of the worlds or the enemy's perspective, will bring us much hope. No matter what challenges we deal with in this life, if we continue to look up, like Minnie has to do every day, we will see things from a different perspective, a heavenly one.

> Dear Heavenly Father, we thank You for giving us hope through Your Son, Jesus Christ. Thank You for forgiving us of all our sins and for the gift of salvation and eternal life with You after we've surrendered our lives to You. Please help us to see things in life through Your perspective. Help us to continually look up and see things as You see them. We are thankful for all You have given us, and it is in Your precious Son's name we pray. Amen.

WHO IS TRAINING WHO?

It's been a long time since I trained a puppy. Back in the 1980s, I raised a golden retriever. I got her when she was only six weeks old. I don't remember her being as hard to train as Minnie. Maybe that's because she had a bigger brain than Minnie does or maybe it's just operator error on my end. Some days with Minnie, I question who is training who.

Minnie has what I call "selective hearing." She listens to me when it is something that she wants to do, like going outside to play or when I have a treat for her. But, if I am trying to get her to do something she doesn't want to do, she acts like she doesn't hear me at all, even though her actions say something else. For example, when I try to put her in her kennel for a nap in the afternoon, she will run into the living room and get in her playpen. Her playpen is more than an arm's length deep, about four feet. She will go as far as she can from the opening and lay down. She thinks that will get me to give up and not make her take a nap. What she fails to remember is that her playpen has a top which can be zipped. So, when I unzip the top, I can reach in and pick her up. Every single time I do that, Minnie acts as though it is the first time she has ever seen me do that. Once I've picked her up, I can carry her to her kennel for a nap and as a result, she doesn't get her way and my command to take a nap prevails.

I really can't get mad at her when she does that because I know that I all too often do that with God. I'm happy to listen to God when He is wanting to bless me or lead me down a path I enjoy being on. But, when He wants me to listen to Him as

He directs me to a different path, one that I don't really want to be on, I, too, can run as far into a corner as I can and hope He doesn't see me and then I won't have to do what He is asking of me. The hardest thing that God has asked of me is to live my life without my late husband. Being a widow is something that my friends, who are also widows, say is a club that none of us wanted to join but God had other plans for us. God is training us how to live a life dependent on Him, instead of our late husbands. Some days this training goes smoothly, while other days are quite challenging. One thing I have learned is that God will always get His way, whether I like it or not. It's just like with Minnie and me, I will always get my way because I know what is best for her. And in Jeremiah 29:11, we are told that God's plans for us are indeed good.

God trains and guides us through His Word. 2 Timothy 3:16-17 tells us of the importance of scripture. "All scripture is inspired by God and profitable for teaching, for reproof, for correction, for training in righteousness; so that the man of God may be adequate, equipped for every good work." God's Word is there to help us live a life pleasing to Him and a life that is in turn, good for us.

There is a huge difference between how I train Minnie and how God trains us. With Minnie, her training is truly a work in progress. As I see that one training tactic doesn't work with her, I try a different one. Sometimes I have to try several ways before I find the best way to get Minnie to do what I want her to do on a regular basis. Unfortunately, it is more of a trial-and-error type of approach with her training. Sometimes it is confusing to Minnie when I try a new training method. But when we find something that works, we stick to it. Thankfully, God doesn't do that with us. He already knows what works and what doesn't and that is one reason His Word never changes. It doesn't have to. Hebrews 13:8 confirms that when it says, "Jesus Christ is the same yesterday and today and forever." And if He doesn't change, neither does

His Word. With God, we can be one hundred percent certain that if things in our lives aren't going in the right direction, the change needed to be made to make things right will always be with us, not God. There is so much comfort knowing that God and His Word will always remain the same. It is a firm, never-shifting foundation that we can build on day by day.

The rules I have for Minnie are put into place for her good. She enjoys life so much more when she is well rested, thus the reason I make her take a nap. God does the same thing with us. His rules found throughout scripture are put there for our good. God wants the very best for us. It is always in our best interest to follow His commands. Whether or not we agree with the path that God has us on, we can be assured that we are on it for a good reason, even if we don't understand why. Our job is to obey God's commands and let Him be the One who is training us, not us trying to train Him by telling Him to want we want.

> Dear Heavenly Father, we thank you for training us in Your Word. We might not always understand the "why" behind what You are doing, but we can trust in the way You are training us. We thank you for being a never-changing God. We find security in the way You lead and guide us. Thank You that we have not only Your Word but the Holy Spirit to help us as we learn to do things so they will be pleasing to You and beneficial to us. May we always yield to Your direction as You take us down the paths You have laid out for us, and it is in Your Son's precious name we pray. Amen.

LOVING CARE

Never giving birth to any children of my own, there hasn't been a time in my life that I was the only one responsible for another life, until now. So having Minnie depend on me for all her needs is pretty cool. When I was making my list of pros and cons during the decision-making process of whether or not to get a dog, having someone who would depend on me was in the pro column. Someone to love and to be loved by was also in the pro column. Minnie depends on me for her food, shelter, medical care and most importantly, love. You know, the basic things in life.

I'm not the only one who loves on Minnie. Others that spend time with Minnie also show her love. My niece and nephew and their three girls have kept Minnie for me when I was not able to care for her and Minnie loves them too. My youngest great-niece here in Texas calls herself a "dog whisperer" and I would have to agree with that title. Some of my favorite pictures of Minnie are those with my great-nieces. There is just something about young life loving on young life that touches my heart.

Something else that also touches my heart is the way God cares for all our needs. He tells us that we do not need to worry about our basic needs because not only does God know what we need, He has promised to take care of all those needs. Matthew 6:25-33 tells us about this in Jesus' own words:

> For this reason I say to you, do not be worried about your life, as to what you will eat or what you will drink; nor for your body, as to what you will put on. Is not life more

than food, and the body more than clothing? Look at the birds of the air, that they do not sow, nor reap nor gather into barns, and yet your heavenly Father feeds them. Are you not worth much more than they? And who of you by being worried can add a single hour to his life? And why are you worried about clothing? Observe how the lilies of the field grow; they do not toil nor do they spin, yet I say to you that not even Solomon in all his glory clothed himself like one of these. But if God so clothes the grass of the field, which is alive today and tomorrow is thrown into the furnace, will He not much more clothe you? You of little faith! Do not worry then, saying, 'What will we eat?' or 'What will we drink?' or 'What will we wear for clothing?' For the Gentiles eagerly seek all these things; for your heavenly Father knows that you need all these things. But seek first His kingdom and His righteousness, and all these things will be added to you.

Jesus is saying that if we seek His kingdom and His righteousness, He will provide everything we need. Are we not more valuable than birds? Jesus says that we are! That is a truth that we need to remind ourselves of often. WE ARE VALUABLE TO GOD! Do you believe that? God wants us to believe that truth so much that there is only one place in the Bible where He tells us to test Him on this truth. Malachi 3:8-12 says it like this:

> Would anyone rob God? Yet you are robbing Me! But you say, 'How have we robbed You?' In tithes and offerings. You are cursed with a curse, for you are robbing Me, the entire nation of you! Bring the whole tithe into the storehouse, so that there may be food in My house, and put Me to the test now in this," says the Lord of armies, "if I do not open for you the windows of heaven and pour out for you a blessing until it overflows. Then I will rebuke the devourer for you, so that it will not destroy the fruit of your ground; nor will the vine in the field prove fruitless to you," says the Lord of armies. "All the nations will call you blessed, for you will be a delightful land," says the Lord of armies."

In other words, it was like Jesus was telling us to test Him on this. He could have said, "Trust me to provide for your needs and see if I don't open the windows of heaven and provide for everything you need.

Can the Lord provide for everyone? Absolutely! Exodus 19:5 tells us that all "all the earth is Mine." Psalm 50:10 tells us more about what God owns. "Every beast of the forest is Mine, the cattle on a thousand hills." "Mine" meaning God has every resource on earth available for His use any way He likes. God's resources are unlimited so there is no reason for us to ever feel like God can't provide what we need. Take Minnie for example. I was wanting a dog to fill a need in my life. Unfortunately, her previous owner could no longer take care of her. So, God changed owners for Minnie and blessed me by filling a longing of my heart. And at the same time, God took care of Minnie's previous owner's need to find his puppy a new home.

Two of my favorite verses dealing with God taking care of our needs are Philippians 4:19 and Ephesians 3:20. "And my God will supply all your needs according to His riches in glory in Christ Jesus." And ALL means ALL! "Now to Him who is able to do far more abundantly beyond all that we ask or think, according to the power that works within us, to Him be the glory in the church and in Christ Jesus to all generations forever and ever. Amen." From small things like getting a pet to larger things like healing us from diseases, those are two amazing promises that we can stand on every single day for all generations to come! God has our needs covered. We just need to trust Him.

Dear Heavenly Father, we thank you for being our Provider. You always know our needs before we do and You are faithful to fulfill Your promise to provide all that we need. Holy Spirit, please help us to always seek the kingdom of God and His righteousness first and foremost in life. You love us more than words can say and Your actions show us that daily. May our love for You be just as evident by how we live our life for Your glory. In Your Son's precious name we pray. Amen.

WHAT WOULD YOU PAY?

As I told you in the first chapter of this book, I searched for the perfect puppy a long time before God brought me Minnie. Some of the ads for puppies were just crazy because of the prices they were asking. I love dogs, but the Lord knew my budget wouldn't allow me to spend thousands of dollars to get one. The most expensive puppy I saw advertised was priced over $5,000. At the bottom of the ad, it said to not reply unless you were a serious buyer. For that price, I was seriously sure that I would not be buying that puppy!

God knew my budget and what I could afford. When I went to pick up Minnie from her previous owner, I was prepared to pay for her, but God had another plan. The owner wasn't interested in me paying anything for her. He just wanted to know that she was going to a good home where she would be loved and cared for. What a blessing that was for me!! God knew what I desired, and He brought Minnie to me in a way I could afford…free! Minnie is truly one of the greatest gifts I've ever received.

The greatest gift I've ever received was also free. Well, it was free for me. I'll get back to that in a moment. Let me ask you a question. What would you pay to spend eternity in heaven with God the Father, God the Son, and God the Holy Spirit? $5,000? $10,000? $100,000? More? Before you answer that question, let me tell you a little bit about my Savior, Jesus Christ.

The Lord is omniscient. He knows everything. Everything that has happened. Everything that is happening now. Everything about you. And everything that will happen in the future.

Psalm 147:5 says, "Great is our Lord and abundant in strength; His understanding is infinite." I am blessed to serve a God that has total understanding of everything.

The Lord is omnipresent. He is everywhere all at the same time. That is mind-boggling for me. How cool is it that He is where you currently are, as well as in other parts of the world that you can't see, all at the same time! Psalm 139:7-12 expands that thought:

> Where can I go from Your Spirit? Or where can I flee from Your presence?
> If I ascend to heaven, You are there; if I make my bed in Sheol, behold, You are there. If I take the wings of the dawn, if I dwell in the remotest part of the sea, even there Your hand will lay hold of me. If I say, 'Surely the darkness will overwhelm me, and the light around me will be night,' even the darkness is not dark to You, and the night is as bright as the day. Darkness and light are alike to You.

God is everywhere. There is not a spot on this earth, not even one, where He can't be found. And not just be found but be found everywhere at the same time. Now that is an impressive God!

The Lord is also omnipotent. He is infinitely powerful, enough to meet your every need. Philippians 4:19 gives us a promise we can stand firm on. "And my God will supply all your needs according to His riches in glory in Christ Jesus." And when God says He will supply ALL your needs, all means just that, ALL.

Now let's get back to the question I asked you earlier. What would you pay to spend eternity in heaven with God the Father, God the Son, and God the Holy Spirit? What would it be worth to you to have the Lord walking and talking with you everywhere you go right here on earth? And does knowing that God promises to meet all your needs make Him more valuable to you than anyone or anything else in your life? The good news is that it doesn't cost you anything to become a child of God. The gift

of salvation is a gift from God through Jesus to assure that all of these things and more can indeed be yours.

Since we are all sinners, we have a sin debt problem. No matter how much good we did in our lives, it still would not be enough to pay the debt we would owe God. Since God knew that, He sent His Son, Jesus Christ, to satisfy that debt for us. John 3:16 says, "For God so loved the world, that He gave His only begotten Son, that whoever believes in Him shall not perish, but have eternal life." Jesus paid our total sin debt when He died on the cross in our place. He satisfied our sin debt and covered all our sins – past, present, and future sins. The gift of salvation is a gift that just keeps on giving. It puts us in right standing with God. It allows us to experience a taste of heaven while we are still on earth. This amazing gift makes us a child of God and allows us to have a personal relationship with Him. I would say that these things are absolutely priceless, and they didn't cost you a penny. Jesus paid it all! And once again, ALL means just that. ALL!!

> Dear Heavenly Father, thank You that You loved us enough that You sent Your only Son, Jesus, to pay for the sin debt that we could never pay for ourselves. While this gift didn't cost us a dime, the cost to You and Your Son was great. Knowing exactly what the cost would be, You still chose to provide this gift of salvation. This gift is something we are eternally grateful for. Help us to experience a close relationship with You while we are still here on earth, and then once You call us home, thank You that we will forever be in Your presence. In Your Son's precious name we pray. Amen.

WHAT A TREASURE!

Minnie is such a treasure for me! She loves everything I love, well, almost everything. She likes to sit with me as I do my Bible studies and write devotions. But if she thinks I've spent too much time doing either of these, she will try to swipe my laptop screen or close my book. She loves watching most sports with me. She enjoys tennis, football, and baseball, but not golf. Her ears perk up when she hears me cheer on my favorite teams or players. When I "hoot and holler" when good things happen, she barks right along with me. She loves to play fetch with me and when the weather is agreeable, she enjoys walks through my neighborhood. On those walks, when we encounter other dogs, Minnie forgets that she is a little thing and can't take on larger dogs! Everyone gets a chuckle out of her acting like she's a big dog, well, everyone except Minnie. What Minnie really doesn't like is when I tell her "we" need to take a nap. Oh well, her liking four out of five things isn't bad.

She knows when I'm having a hard day, either emotionally or physically, or sometimes both. On those days, she stays even closer by my side. I love how animals can sense what we need. She is the closest thing I've experienced to unconditional love here on earth since my husband passed away. I don't ever have to explain to her what I need or why I'm sometimes quiet. When I leave her at the house, she responds to me the same way when I get home whether I've been gone ten minutes or a few hours – full of hugs and kisses. It is so nice to have someone to come

home to again. She is truly the treasure that God knew I needed at this time in my life.

God has lots to say about the treasures we have. Jesus gives us instructions about what to do with those treasures in Matthew 6:19-21:

> Do not store up for yourselves treasures on earth, where moth and rust destroy, and where thieves break in and steal. But store up for yourselves treasures in heaven, where neither moth nor rust destroys, and where thieves do not break in or steal; for where your treasure is, there your heart will be also.

This verse doesn't mean that we are not to have material things. Jesus was encouraging His disciples to invest their treasures where their value won't be lost. He was telling them that their hearts would follow what they treasured. If we only focus on acquiring "things," or treasures, Jesus was reminding us that those things can be lost in an instant. Anyone who has ever lost everything because of a tornado, hurricane, or fire will tell you that the most important things that survived these tragedies aren't things at all. The intangible things that moths or rust can't destroy are what truly matter. Our relationships with God, our brothers and sisters in Christ, our family and friends, our faith and those things that go along with living out our faith are the treasures that matter.

God does bless us with material things for our pleasure and to satisfy our physical needs. Minnie is one of those things that God has blessed me with. So are my house, car, and the belongings in my house. God has given me these things to meet my earthly needs and desires. But they are things that I could lose in a moment if I experienced any of those tragedies I listed above. I need to care for the things that God has given me stewardship over while I'm here on earth, but my main focus needs to be on things of the Lord, not things of this earth.

Did you know that as a child of God, you are one of God's treasures? I remember the first time I wrapped my mind around that fact. How cool is it that we are one of the things that the Creator of heaven and earth treasures? I know, right? It is mind-blowing! Here are some of the things that the King of Kings and the Lord of Lords says about you:

- » You are beloved by God and chosen. (1 Thessalonians 1:4)
- » You are created. (Genesis 1:31)
- » You are amazing. (Romans 8:39)
- » You are enough. (2 Corinthians 12:9)
- » You are capable. (Mark 10:27)
- » You are strong. (Philippians 4:13)
- » You are beautiful. (Ecclesiastes 3:11)
- » And one of my favorites – You are NEVER alone. (Matthew 28:20)

Since God says all these things and more about us, we never have to question our worth. We are His treasures!

Dear Heavenly Father, thank You for the things on earth that You have blessed us with to meet our basic needs and desires. Please help us to keep our focus on the treasures that moths and rust can't destroy. We thank You for treasures of heaven that we will one day experience being a child of Yours. While we are here on earth, may our hearts stay focused on those heavenly treasures. We pray these things in Jesus' precious name. Amen.

HOW CLOSE CAN YOU GET?

    Minnie wants to be as close to me as she can get all the time. It amuses me of the way she wiggles to get as close as possible when I've invited her to sit in my recliner with me. When I am not in the recliner, she follows me from room to room as I'm taking care of things in my home. She is really good at letting me know when I am not paying enough attention to her. She has a special high-pitched bark that she only uses when she thinks I am ignoring her. That is not something I trained her to do. It is just an instinctive thing, something that God supplied her with and something she does not hesitate to use.

    God loves to be close with us, just like Minnie loves to be close to me. There is a big difference between how God and Minnie react to me. When I'm not paying enough attention to Minnie, she does not take "no" for an answer. She will pester me until I give up and stop what I am doing so I can give her the attention she is demanding. As much as God wants us to experience His closeness, He doesn't force Himself on us as Minnie does to me. He doesn't wiggle His way in, forcing us to take notice that He is there with us. Instead, He just waits for us to acknowledge Him. Did you catch that? God is always there with us; He just waits for us to recognize that fact. I love how scripture says this in James 4:8. "Draw near to God and He will draw near to you." It is quite humbling when we realize that God wants to draw near to us. He doesn't owe us anything, yet He desires

to be close to us. What a blessing that is! But as the beginning of that scripture says, we first must draw near to Him. It's one of those many "if-then" statements we find in scripture. If, and only if, we do something, then the Lord will do the "then" part of those statements.

So, how do we draw closer to God? Let me answer that question with another question. How do you become good friends with someone? You spend time with them, right? Growing up, we were told to pick our friends wisely because when you spend lots of time with someone, you become more like them. The same is true with God. The more you "hang out" with the Lord, the more you will become like Him. 2 Corinthians 3:18 says it this way: "But we all, with unveiled face, beholding as in a mirror the glory of the Lord, are being transformed into the same image from glory to glory, just as from the Lord, the Spirit." Spending time every day with the Lord helps us become more like Him. Just as new friendships don't evolve over night, becoming more like Jesus takes time.

King David, described by Jesus as "a man after God's own heart," explains what our desire should be in this life. Psalm 27:4 tells us what David desired: "One thing I have asked from the Lord, that I shall seek: that I may dwell in the house of the Lord all the days of my life, to behold the beauty of the Lord and to meditate in His temple." David's desire, which should also be our desire, is that he would have an intimate, life-long relationship with the Lord. He wanted to abide in the Lord's presence all the days of his life. Those types of relationships take time. They grow deeper as we spend more time with Him.

If God is in heaven and we are still on earth, how can we spend time with Him? One of the first things we can do is spend time in God's Word. When we do that, we learn about His character and who He is. In the same way, Minnie and I are learning more about each other as we spend time together. The more time we spend learning about who God is through His Word, the

closer we will become to Him. The more we know about God, the more we will see ourselves changing into His image.

For the past ten years, besides writing five books, I have been writing daily devotions that I text out to many people, and also post on my Facebook page. Over the years, I have been asked how I can come up with something new to write about each day and where my examples come from. The truth is that I don't come up with what I write. The Lord shows me what He would like me to write about. He shows me how He is in the day-to-day details of our life. He then either reminds me of a truth that is already familiar to me, or He teaches me something new about Himself. In my life, this is where the scene from James 4:8 that I referenced earlier takes place. Because I want to learn more about Him and draw closer to Him, God has been faithful to draw closer to me and that is where my ability to write comes from.

No matter where we are in our faith journey, we can always draw closer to God. As we make drawing closer to Him a priority in our lives, we will better understand how much He loves us, wants the best for us, and the great lengths He was willing to go to for us to have the opportunity to become His child.

> Dear Heavenly Father, thank You that we know there is always something new that we can learn about You. And thank You that we also know You keep Your promises. Just like James 4:8 promises, when we draw closer to You, You in turn draw closer to us. Help us to learn as much as we can about You so we can then share that knowledge about You with others. With much gratitude, we pray these things in Your Son's precious name. Amen.

AND THE BATTLE IS ON

Training Minnie often feels like a bunch of small battles. Some battles are won easily, while others are rather difficult to win. I want Minnie to be a well-mannered dog that doesn't jump up on people, bite their hands, or lick their toes. Because that is how I want her to behave, training is an ongoing thing. There have been times that I think she is fully trained in one of those specific areas and that we have won that battle, but then suddenly, she begins acting as though I have never trained her at all. When that happens, I ask her if she behaves that way because she is a tiny dog with a tiny brain. She always turns her head to the side like she has no idea what I'm saying. What Minnie must understand is that while she might win a few small battles during our training times, I **will** win the war.

The same can be said about our Christian faith. The enemy may win a few small battles in our life, but **God** will win the war! Since He is sovereign, the victory belongs to God and God alone for those whom He calls His children. One of the biggest differences between how God directs and trains us in His righteousness and how I train Minnie in good behavior is that God will never change. He directs every event in our life and makes it a part of our story. With Minnie, sometimes I get tired and let her have her way even when it is the opposite of how I am training her. Doing this only sets us back a step with her training, but with God, we know that He never gets tired. He is true to His words found in scripture and He always keeps His promises. Romans 8:28 says it this way. "And we know that

God causes all things to work together for good to those who love God, to those who are called according to His purpose." I need to become more like God as I train Minnie and not give in to her because I know what's best for her. She may not like what I make her do, but it is in her best interest that I do those things. I too need to work out all things for Minnie's good, just like the Lord does for us.

Sometimes it is hard for us to understand what God is doing in our lives. We don't get why He allows pain and heartache when He could stop it all. But then I remember, He could have stopped Jesus dying on the cross to cover our sins, but He didn't. Even allowing His own Son, Jesus, to be the payment for our sin debt was allowed for our good. Without that event happening, we would never be able to be in right standing with God because there is no way we could ever "earn" our way into heaven because our sins could not have been forgiven. If God was willing to go to those great lengths for us, then we have nothing to complain about, even when pain and heartache touch our life.

So, what do we do when those unwanted things pop up in our lives, those things that we do not understand? We might not understand the present happenings, but we can look back at the things that God has already done in our lives. We must realize that we are fighting a battle that God has already won. And if God has already won our battle, we don't have to fight it ourselves. Exodus 14:14 says it like this. "The LORD will fight for you while you keep silent." And Psalm 46:10 says, "Cease striving and know that I am God." That means that if God is handling all the situations in our lives, and He is, we don't have to be fearful, anxious, discouraged or overwhelmed with the circumstances in life.

We see that promise played out in the story found in Exodus 14. The people of Israel were being chased by the Egyptian army. As the Israelites were running away from the Egyptians, they ran out of land as they stood at the shores of the Red Sea. They knew

that the Egyptians were right behind them. Can you imagine the fear and anxiety they must have felt? But God had a plan that they could not have envisioned. Moses told them that they needed to wait on God and that He would work even that dismal situation out for their good and His glory. They needed to just be still. Easier said than done as the Egyptian army was closing in on them. So as the story continues, God rescued the Israelites by parting the Red Sea so that they were able to safely cross over to the other side. But when the Egyptians tried to cross over the parted Red Sea using the same path as the Israelites used, God covered them with the water of the Red Sea, and as a result, they didn't make it to the other side.

Just as we read in this story of how God rescued the Israelites, we are reminded that nothing can ever happen to us that will be beyond the scope of God's sovereign and loving care. He has us in His tender loving hands, and because of that fact, we can rest in Him and be still because He has control over everything. He is our sovereign God and that means that He has already won our battles.

> Dear Heavenly Father, thank You that You are sovereign. Thank You that we know You are working all things for our good, so we don't have to be anxious or fearful of anything. Just like Your word says, we need to just be still and know You are God. We might not totally understand what You may be doing, but we can be confident that You are working all things out and that the victory is Yours. Thankful that we don't need to fight a battle that You have already won. In Your Son's precious name we pray. Amen.

LOCATION, LOCATION, LOCATION

No matter where I take Minnie, she is confident that I am her human. Whether I take her to the vet, the groomer, my sister's, or niece's homes, when I come back to get her, she comes running to me when she sees me. She knows that I love her and will care for her, even if I must physically leave her with others from time to time.

For those who have placed their faith in Jesus Christ, we are His no matter what our location is. I have brothers and sisters in Christ all over the world, not just in the United States. As believers, whether here in the US, Pakistan, Uganda, Myanmar, Puerto Rico, Haiti, or other countries across this world, we all worship and serve the same God and we all belong to the family of God.

Matthew 28:20 gives us directions to the lifestyle we should be living for Him. Jesus said the following in what is known as The Great Commission:

> All authority has been given to Me in heaven and on earth. Go therefore and make disciples of all the nations, baptizing them in the name of the Father and the Son and the Holy Spirit, teaching them to observe all that I commanded you; and lo, I am with you always, even to the end of the age.

God has called us all to be missionaries with the purpose of building His Kingdom. Many of us will not be called to travel to the other side of the world to spread the good news of Jesus

Christ, but we have all been called to be missionaries wherever God has placed us. That could be with your families, neighbors, co-workers or maybe even a stranger that God puts in your path. It doesn't matter where you have been placed. It's not where you are that matters; it is WHO you are in Christ that matters.

It is because of who we are as believers that we can share the gospel with others. Sometimes we are asked to just plant a seed through an act of kindness or lending a compassionate ear to someone who just needs to be heard. Maybe you are asked to share scripture with someone who is looking for answers. You might be asked to share your "faith" story of how you came to ask Jesus to be your Lord and Savior.

Here is the big difference between how Minnie knows that I am her human and who we are in Jesus Christ. I must physically leave Minnie when I go to work or when I take her places, like to the groomers. When I am not with her, she doesn't see my presence. It takes me physically returning before she thinks about me again. She does what other people tell her to do in my absence but seems a little confused about me not being with her at that moment. With God, He never leaves us…never! We might not physically see Him, but His footprints are everywhere. We just have to look for them.

When we are in the midst of a crisis, He is with us. When we are feeling lonely, He is with us. When we are having the best day of our lives, He is with us. When we lose a loved one, He is with us. When new life is brought into this world, He is with us. No matter what the situation is, He is with us. God must have known how much we were going to need the reminder that He is with us, because many scriptures deal with that one single, highly important truth. Here are just a few of the many scriptures that deal with the Lord never leaving or forsaking us:

"Be strong and courageous, do not be afraid or tremble at them, for the LORD your God is the one who goes with you; He will never leave you nor forsake you."
— Deuteronomy 31:6

"No one will be able to stand against you all the days of your life. As I was with Moses, so I will be with you; I will never leave you nor forsake You."
— Joshua 1:5

"Have I not commanded you? Be strong and courageous. Do not be afraid; do not be discouraged, for the LORD your God will be with you wherever you go."
— Joshua 1:9

Wherever you go, God will be with you. He will never leave you or forsake you, not even for a single minute. How comforting is that? Once we say "YES" to Jesus' invitation to be our Lord and Savior, from that moment forward, He will never leave us or forsake us. That promise should bring us so much joy!

Dear Heavenly Father, thank You for the promise that You will never leave or forsake us. You are with us throughout every moment of our life. Thank You that we can stand on Your promises. Wherever You send us to bring hope to others, we can confidently know that You will be going there with us. In Your Son's precious name we pray. Amen.

HIDE AND SEEK

Minnie doesn't do a good job of hiding things when she has done something wrong. For example, she loves to dig in my flower gardens. One such time, I had let her out in my fenced in backyard for her to take care of her business. When I went to let her back inside, I couldn't find her at first. That meant only one thing to me. She was digging in the flower bed behind the four-foot decorative grass in the corner of the flower garden. I called her and when she didn't come, that only confirmed my thoughts on what she had been doing. I walked over to the decorative grass and there she was. I asked her if she had been digging in my flower bed. If looks could speak, she was saying, "Who me? No, I am not digging!" "Oh really," I said. "Then why is mud falling off your face?" You see, Minnie is a blonde Morkie, but on that day, her face and paws were black. She didn't like the bath she immediately got to return her to a blonde. But as I told her, anytime you try to come back inside and are a different color than when you went out, it's bath time!

Inside my house, Minnie has a different approach to her mischievousness. As I told you in an earlier chapter, Minnie loves stealing socks and any paper product that she can. I always know when she has something she shouldn't have because she runs to her playpen and goes to the furthest spot from the opening, where she thinks I can't reach her. Every time she does that, she finds out that I can indeed reach her. She's a slow learner sometimes.

We, too, try to hide our sins from God, but that is impossible because He sees everything and knows about everything in our life. Take Adam and Eve for example, the first two people to sin. We read about that story in the third chapter of Genesis:

> Now the serpent was more cunning than any animal of the field which the Lord God had made. And he said to the woman, "Has God really said, 'You shall not eat from any tree of the garden?'" The woman said to the serpent, "From the fruit of the trees of the garden we may eat; but from the fruit of the tree which is in the middle of the garden, God has said, 'You shall not eat from it or touch it, or you will die.'" The serpent said to the woman, "You certainly will not die! For God knows that on the day you eat from it your eyes will be opened, and you will become like God, knowing good and evil." When the woman saw that the tree was good for food, and that it was a delight to the eyes, and that the tree was desirable to make one wise, she took some of its fruit and ate; and she also gave some to her husband with her, and he ate. Then the eyes of both of them were opened, and they knew that they were naked; and they sewed fig leaves together and made themselves waist coverings. Now they heard the sound of the Lord God walking in the garden in the cool of the day, and the man and his wife hid themselves from the presence of the Lord God among the trees of the garden. Then the Lord God called to the man, and said to him, "Where are you?" He said, "I heard the sound of You in the garden, and I was afraid because I was naked; so I hid myself." And He said, "Who told you that you were naked? Have you eaten from the tree from which I commanded you not to eat?" The man said, "The woman whom You gave to be with me, she gave me some of the fruit of the tree, and I ate." Then the Lord God said to the woman, "What is this that you have done?" And the woman said, "The serpent deceived me and I ate."

And right there was the first instance of someone blaming something they did on someone else. But just as I don't accept that when Minnie tries to hide her sneakiness from me, God did not accept their explanation when Adam and Eve tried to blame the sin on the serpent and take no personal responsibility of giving into the temptation.

The most important element of this story is what God did for Adam and Eve after He caught them in their sin. He reprimanded them and expelled them from the garden to work for the food they ate instead of being able to eat the food the Lord provided for them in the garden. But here's my favorite part. Verse 21 says, "The LORD God made garments of skin for Adam and his wife and clothed them." Yes, they sinned and there were consequences to their sin but God, being the compassionate Father that He is, clothed them. He provided for their basic needs.

God wants to provide us with what we need. But when we do sin, and yes, we are all going to sin, we can turn to God, confess our sins, and then let Him restore us. We are not free from the consequences of our sin, but God desires to restore us to Him. God understands our temptations. Hebrews 4:15-16 says it like this: "For we do not have a high priest who cannot sympathize with our weaknesses, but One who has been tempted in all things as we are, yet without sin. Therefore let us draw near with confidence to the throne of grace, so that we may receive mercy and find grace to help in time of need." When we sin, we don't have to run and try to hide from God. We don't need to try to blame someone else for our sin. It is a waste of time to hope that God won't know what you did, because He is everywhere you are and knows everything you do. Instead, we need to run to God for His help… help He always wants to give you.

> Dear Heavenly Father, thank You that You understand when we are tempted and fall into sin. Thank You for Your forgiveness that You give us through Jesus Christ. Please help us to not give in to temptation but bring those challenges to You for help. We ask these things in Your Son's precious name. Amen.

HAIR, HAIR AND MORE HAIR

    Minnie is a hypoallergenic dog, which is good for my lungs, but she still sheds hair. Those that know me well, know that I like things nice and tidy, including my house. Having Minnie has definitely helped me be less concerned about having a totally clean house all the time. If I see her hair on the floor, I will sweep the floor when time allows, which means it might not happen until tomorrow and that is okay with me. It is more important to me to spend time playing with Minnie instead of cleaning my house daily. Let's just say that I have a new appreciation for moms with small children at home.

    Besides finding Minnie's hair in my house, she did something that I am told puppies usually don't do. She brought me one of her puppy teeth when it fell out. She was so proud of herself to present that little tooth to me. She has done that twice. I asked her if she thought I was a tooth fairy. When I looked into her mouth, I could not see where she had lost those two teeth and I don't know when she lost them. She could have hidden them for a while before she brought them to me. I don't know everything about Minnie, like how many teeth she has, but we serve a God that knows us well. In both Luke 12:7 and Matthew 10:30-31, Jesus tells us that He knows everything about us, even the number of hairs on our head. Isn't that something that the Creator of heaven and earth knows those details about us? I shouldn't be surprised that He knows every detail about us since He created us.

Have you ever wondered why God created you? It's an age-old question. What is the meaning of life? I'm sure that question has been asked since the beginning of time. And I am also sure that many different answers have been given to explain why God created you. As a believer in Jesus Christ, we already know the answer to that question. There are literally a hundred different scriptures in the Bible that will answer that question. I think the one that states it the clearest is found in Isaiah 43:7. It says: "Everyone who is called by My name, and whom I have created for My glory, whom I have formed, even whom I have made." That's the answer. Plain and simple. God created us for His glory! We weren't created to glorify ourselves, as many do in this fallen world. We were created for His glory. Does that make you sit up a little taller knowing that you are able to glorify Him?

How then do we give God glory? First and foremost, we praise Him for who He is, what He has done, and what He will do in the future. It is easy to praise God when we are on top of the world and everything in our life is going great, but what about when life is challenging? Are we asked to praise God then, too? The answer to that question is a resounding, "YES!" It may not be as easy to do, but God will lift you up when you praise Him in the tough times.

Another way to glorify God is found in 1 Corinthians 10:31. That verse says, "Whether then, you eat or drink or whatever you do, do all to the glory of God." That verse reminds us that no matter what we do in life, we should do it in a way that brings God glory. People who have not yet become a child of God, by asking Him to be their Lord and Savior, watch what Christians do. They look to see if their words and actions match. Are Christians living a life that would draw others to God? Does the non-believer see something different in them, and as a result, want to experience what the believer has? If they do, they are successfully glorifying God.

Ephesians 2:10 gives us another way we can glorify God: "For we are His workmanship, created in Christ Jesus for good works, which God prepared beforehand so that we would walk in them." Before we were even born, God created good works that we could do for Him. If you have ever felt like your life didn't matter, think about this. God made you part of His plan for the redemption of all mankind. I know you are sitting up straighter now! God chose to use you! He created good works for you to do as you go through your days. The next time you do a good work, you might want to stop and thank God for creating that opportunity for you. If God wants to use you and your life situations to do good things for others, it doesn't matter what anyone else has to say about anything. You are loved and used by God! It doesn't get any better than that. Matthew 5:16 elaborates on that thought of doing good works to bring God glory. Jesus Himself spoke these words: "Let your light shine before men in such a way that they may see your good works, and glorify your Father who is in heaven."

We might not know everything about our Creator, but we do know the most important things. God created us for His glory and our lives should glorify Him in all we say and do. God knows every detail in our life, even the number of hairs on our head, and we never have to question again why we were created. It's all about God and His glory!

> Dear Heavenly Father, thank You for clearly giving us the reason why we were created. You know every detail of our lives and love us unconditionally. Being Your child, our desire is to bring You the glory we were created for. Please help us to bring You glory in all we say and do. Help us to shine our light so others see You in and through our lives. And may others be drawn to You as we carry out the good works You have prepared for us to do. We pray all these things in Your Son's precious name. Amen.

TO BE OR NOT TO BE ... CONTENT THAT IS??!!

One of the things that amuses me about Minnie has to do with her toys. I only give her a few toys to play with at a time. I swap in and out other toys when it seems like she has become bored with one or more of her current toys. Instead of just playing with one toy at a time, she does her best to put as many toys in her mouth all at once. She literally will spend an hour at a time trying to get them all in her mouth. She will get two in her mouth without much effort and occasionally, she can get three toys in her mouth after she works on it for a while. But she will wear herself out trying to get four toys in her mouth at one time. As far as I know, she has only once been successful with getting four toys in her mouth at one time. She found a way to put a pickleball, a small tennis ball, a rope toy and her "baby" in her mouth at the same time. I wasn't able to get a picture of her doing this, but what I can tell you is that not even the most skilled chipmunk could not have outdone Minnie!

We are a lot like Minnie in this regard. We often wear ourselves out trying to get more and more in life. Working longer hours to make more money so we can buy those things that help us keep up with what others have. The bottom line is that we aren't satisfied with what we have and therefore, we want more. Instead of being content with what we have, we spend lots of time and money and often make bad decisions trying to enhance what we already have.

Having an eternal perspective on this topic is critical. If you just listen to what the world has to say about being content, you will feel like you must work much harder to get more and more. Just turn your television on and watch the commercials that encourage you to buy, buy, and buy some more. The commercials want you to believe that you deserve whatever they are selling and some of them try to make you feel guilty if you don't buy what they are selling. The allure of greed runs rampant in our world today.

1 Timothy 6:6-8 instructs us on how to be content in this world today: "But godliness actually is a means of great gain when accompanied by contentment. For we have brought nothing into this world, so we cannot take anything out of it either. If we have food and covering, with these we shall be content." Could you see yourself being content with just food and clothing? With God, it's possible. We are told that we should not have a love of money in Hebrews 13:5: "Make sure that your character is free from the love of money, being content with what you have; for He Himself has said, "I WILL NEVER DESERT YOU, NOR WILL I EVER FORSAKE YOU."

In the book of Luke (Luke 12:15), Jesus teaches us that we need to guard against greed. He said, "Beware, and be on your guard against every form of greed; for not even when one has an abundance does his life consist of his possessions." In other words, what we own should not define us. One day when we stand before the Lord, He won't be asking us what we have accumulated in our earthly life. He will be asking us what we did with the resources we were given to increase the Kingdom of God.

We can be content in every situation in life because our contentment needs to be found in the Lord and Him alone. It shouldn't be based on the things we have or don't have in life. That doesn't mean we should not have any material things. God has provided those things for us but what it means is that we should not place our contentment in life on those things. If we believe that God is in control of our life, and He is, then we can be content even when we find ourselves in difficult situations. The apostle Paul found himself in many difficult situations throughout his time in ministry. In 2 Corinthians 12:7-9, Paul tells us about one of those difficult times: "Because of the surpassing greatness of the revelations, for this reason, to keep me from exalting myself, there was given me a thorn in the flesh, a messenger of Satan to torment me – to keep me from exalting myself! Concerning this I implored the Lord three times that it might leave me. And He has said to me, 'My grace is sufficient for you, for power is perfected in weakness.' Most gladly, therefore, I will rather boast about my weaknesses, so that the power of Christ may dwell in me."

Paul also said this in Philippians 4:11-13, concerning being content: "Not that I speak from want, for I have learned to be content in whatever circumstances I am. I know how to get along with humble means, and I also know how to live in prosperity; in any and every circumstance I have learned the secret of being filled and going hungry, both of having abundance and suffering need. I can do all things through Him who strengthens me." And there it is. Contentment comes from God, and so with God, we can be content in all things, just like Paul said.

> Dear Heavenly Father, we are thankful that we only need You to be content with life. What we have or don't have shouldn't be a factor as to whether we are content or not. One day when we leave this earth, our possessions are left behind. Help us to be content with what You have allowed us to be stewards over. You have promised to take care of our basic needs and everything else is just extra. Please help us grow in You instead of material things that won't mean anything when we die. And when temptations arise inviting us to do things we shouldn't do, just so we can have more, remind us that we are just passing through this world. Help us to see what really matters in this life and help us to put our time, energy and money into those things. It is in Your Son's precious name we pray. Amen.

ROUTINE OR BUST

Routines are a good thing. If Minnie gets off her schedule, she gets really unsettled and can become quite a stinker, but then again, so can I. We have our morning routine: I let her out of her kennel, two trips outside before she starts eating, then play time. I love having this routine with her. The other cute routine she has occurs at night. Minnie likes to take a nap about 30 minutes before she goes to bed. She will sleep for about 20 to 25 minutes, and then she wakes up and wants to cuddle for a few minutes. After cuddle time, I will put her to bed. She is so loving at night. She just wants to lay close to me on my lap or wants me to hold her. During this time, she wants my full attention, and my full attention she gets.

On days that Minnie's routine has been changed, she absolutely does not want to go to bed at night. It has taken a bit for me to figure out what she tries to tell me on those nights and what she needs. We are getting much better with our communication. She truly is like a small child. Instead of going to bed, she wants a drink, then she wants to go outside, and then… Well, you get the idea. It is on those nights where I have to spend more time with her than normal and eventually, she will wear herself out and go to sleep. And by that time, I am ready for bed, too!

Just like Minnie, I need a routine. When my days get hectic, and something has to be sacrificed, the last thing I will change about my day is being in God's Word. Reading the Bible is my direct communication with God and especially when I am frazzled from a day with no routine, I absolutely need a word from

Him. I will study God's Word at some point during the day, but at night, I read His Word to calm my mind, body, and soul. It settles me like nothing else can.

There are lots of scriptures dealing with the importance of God's Word. Here are just a few of my favorites:

Hebrews 4:12 says: "For the word of God is living and active and sharper than any two-edged sword, and piercing as far as the division of soul and spirit, of both joints and marrow, and able to judge the thoughts and intention of the heart."

In Matthew 4:4, Jesus Himself also tells us why the Word of God is important for us to have:

"It is written, 'Man shall not live on bread alone, but on every word that proceeds out of the mouth of God.'" We need God's Word as much as we need food to survive this life, and God has provided answers for everything in His Word.

Psalm 119:105 is a good verse for me because I am a visual learner, and it paints a picture for me of the importance of staying in God's Word: "Your word is a lamp to my feet and a light to my path." We need a light in the darkness and God's Word is that light for us.

And John 1:1-4 says: "In the beginning was the Word, and the Word was with God, and the Word was God. He was in the beginning with God. All things came into being through Him, and apart from Him nothing came into being that has come into being. In Him was life, and the life was the Light of men." God and His Word are the same thing. So, when I read His Word, I am communicating with Him. And at the end of a stressful day, there is no one better to be talking with.

There are many benefits of staying in God's Word. One would be that God's Word brings us joy, and who couldn't use more joy in their life??!! When something goes terribly wrong in my day, I turn to His Word so I can experience His joy instead of the chaos happening in my life. Besides that, God's Word also gives me free counseling. Reading His Word lets me know what

He has to say about a particular problem. The enemy wants me to call someone so they can tell me what to do, but I have found over the years, when I have a problem, there is always something God has to say about it in His Word. For every lie the enemy tries to get me to believe, there are multiple things that God says to combat the enemy's lie. So you see, God's Word has become my anchor in life, and it brings me hope in difficult situations. Hebrews 6:19 says it this way: "This hope we have as an anchor of the soul, and hope both sure and steadfast and one which enters within the veil." God goes before us in all things. He knows better than anyone the lies the enemy tries to get us to believe, but by staying in God's Word, we are anchored in His truth. God's truths and promises bring us hope in all things.

> Dear Heavenly Father, life can get really stressful, especially when we take our focus off of You. Your Word is the anchor our soul needs to successfully navigate this life. It is one of the ways we communicate with You. It brings us joy and hope for our days. Your Word is as necessary as the food we eat to sustain us. It guides our paths as we journey through this life. Help us to always find a way in our busy lives to spend time in Your Word. Help us to make communicating with You the most important part of our day's routine so we can thrive in this life with You. It's in Your Son's precious name we pray. Amen.

DO I GET A TREAT FOR THAT?

As a former teacher, I gave my students treats when they would meet a goal or maybe just for some encouragement. As I started to train Minnie, I would use her treats to reward good behavior. I thought I was doing a good job training Minnie, but when she turned six months old, she lost her mind. I can relate her behavior to the "terrible twos" that lots of children go through. She acted and reacted to things like she had had no previous training. This lasted for several weeks, and it was quite discouraging for me. And during this time, every time her behavior was good, she ran to where I had her treats stored. She was a demanding little thing. I found it quite curious that she remembered where her treats were stored but remembered little else. Then, just as quickly as she lost her mind weeks earlier, she returned to her loving and obedient self.

This reminded me of how the Israelites behaved. I lost count of the number of times they lost their minds and turned away from God. Throughout the Old Testament, we see time and time again a pattern of disobedience from the Israelites. God would save them from the enemy and in a short amount of time, they would return to their rebellious ways, ignoring God and forgetting what He had done for them. It is not that the Israelites didn't know better, it was that they didn't follow what they had been taught. In today's world, I'm afraid we are like the Israelites.

We know about God and what He has done for us, but choose to follow the things of this world instead of Him.

We live in a world of instant gratification. With modern technology, everything is just a keystroke away. We want dinner and don't want to cook so we call and have it delivered to our home. We often get irritated if the delivery takes too long to get to us. We get fed without much effort on our part at all. We want what our neighbors have so we spend money that we don't have just to "keep up with the Joneses," as the saying goes. We'll deal with the cost of it later. Something looks appealing to us, and we partake in it, regardless of the consequences. Sound familiar? Yes, it is just like Adam and Eve did in the Garden of Eden. Have we not gotten any further along in our obedience to God than this???

God has a lot to say about being obedient to Him throughout scriptures. John 14:15 tells us how God knows if we love Him or not. Jesus said, "If you love Me, you will keep My commandments." What commandments was He referring to? The Ten Commandments that are given to us in Exodus 20. They are a blueprint of living a Christ-filled life. These are the things that God knew would keep our focus on Him instead of the sin found in our fallen world. But if the Ten Commandments are too hard to wrap our limited minds around, we can turn to Matthew 22:36-40 to narrow down what the Lord commands. Jesus was asked, "'Teacher, which is the great commandment in the Law?' And Jesus responded saying this, 'YOU SHALL LOVE THE LORD YOUR GOD WITH ALL YOUR HEART, AND WITH ALL YOUR SOUL, AND WITH ALL YOUR MIND. This is the great and foremost commandment. The second is like it, YOU SHALL LOVE YOUR NEIGHBOR AS YOURSELF.' On these two commandments depend the whole Law and the Prophets." If we didn't focus on anything but loving God and our neighbors, we would be living a life pleasing to the Lord. It would be the canopy that we could live our lives under. If we are doing these two commandments, we will find that we are also doing all of the ten commandments that God gave us in Exodus.

As important as it is to be obedient by reading God's Word daily, we just can't stop with only reading it. James 1:22 says: "But prove yourselves doers of the Word, and not merely hearers who delude themselves." We have to put what we learn in God's Word into actions. In Luke 6:46-49, we are told why being doers of the Word is so important. Jesus says, "Why do you call Me, 'Lord, Lord,' and do not do what I say? Everyone who comes to Me and hears My words and acts on them, I will show you whom he is like: he is like a man building a house, who dug deep and laid a foundation on the rock; and when a flood occurred, the torrent burst against that house and could not shake it, because it had been built well. But the one who has heard and has not acted accordingly, is like a man who built a house on the ground without any foundation; and the torrent burst against it and immediately it collapsed, and the ruin of that house was great."

Obedience to God leads us to living a life that is pleasing to Him. Life runs so much smoother when we choose to be obedient to what we find in His Word. Just like with Minnie, our life together is so much better when she allows me to train her to do things that make her life safer and more enjoyable. I know when I have achieved success with training Minnie because she no longer wants a treat to do what is right. And for us, doing what is right in the eyes of the Lord should be a reward in itself, too.

> Dear Heavenly Father, thank You for giving us the blueprint on how to live a life that is pleasing to You. Help us to follow Your commandments which not only protect us from a sinful life, but bring You honor and glory. And when we fall short of living that godly life, please forgive us and help us get back on the right path. We pray these things in Your Son's precious name. Amen.

PATIENCE, PATIENCE, AND MORE PATIENCE

Have I mentioned that it takes lots of patience when training a dog? Minnie has been no exception to that rule, but together, we are figuring things out. Some days of training are better than others but having her with me has been a huge blessing each day. God knew exactly what I needed for this chapter of my life, and He provided Minnie in a way that only He could. She is absolutely a perfect companion for me, but God knew she would be. The life and laughter she has brought to my home has been a game changer for me. I am indeed blessed to have her! With that being said, how could I not be patient with her?

I hope that I give Minnie the same patience as God has given me over the years. Just like with Minnie, God and I have always figured things out together. He has been so patient with me throughout my journey with Him. When I am on a mountain top, the Lord has been my biggest cheerleader. When life has brought challenges and I find myself in a low spot, He has been right there to encourage me out of that valley. I am in awe of the way He loves and provides for me. With all my health challenges, He has been there. With the loss of my husband, He has been there. With relationship issues, He has been there. With periods of loneliness, He has been there. With writing daily devotions, He has been there. And with my move to Texas, He was there, too. When I accepted Jesus as my Lord and Savior in 1986, He was there with me and He wants to be there with you, too.

Not only does He want to be with you, but He also wants to save you from the penalty of sin in your life. James 4:14 tells us that we "do not know what your life will be like tomorrow. You are just a vapor that appears for a little while and then vanishes away." So, since we do not know what tomorrow will bring and the exact time that we will leave this earth, we need to take care of the most important decision of our life. Even though God is patient with us and does not want anyone to perish and be separated from Him for all eternity, everyone needs to make the decision where they will spend eternity. Yes, it is our choice!

One of the best known scriptures in the Bible is John 3:16. In this verse, we are clearly told how each of us can spend eternity in heaven with the Lord. "For God so loved the world, that He gave His only begotten Son, that whoever believes in Him shall not perish, but have eternal life." And verse 17 continues that truth. "For God did not send the Son into the world to judge the world, but that the world might be saved through Him."

God has made a way for everyone to be saved through the gift of salvation in His Son, Jesus Christ. All it takes to become a child of God is to accept that God sent Jesus to come and be the payment of our sin debt. We could never do enough good things in this world to pay the penalty we owe God for all of our sins and God knew that. He sent Jesus to pay the price for us. Once we have accepted Jesus Christ as our Lord and Savior, God sees us differently. He sees us as righteous, as the blood of Jesus shed on the cross covers us. He no longer sees our sins because all our sins – past, present, and future – have been forgiven. We now live for the Lord.

If you have already asked Jesus to be your Lord and Savior, I look forward to the day I can meet you in heaven, if I don't already know you. We will have an eternity to get to know each other. If you haven't asked Jesus into your life, I pray that you would not put that eternal decision off another day since we are not guaranteed tomorrow here on earth.

If you don't know how to accept Jesus as your Lord and Savior, pray this prayer with me:

> "Lord, I know that I am a sinner and have a sin debt that I could never repay. I believe that You sent Your Son, Jesus, to die in my place. I believe that Jesus died, was buried, and was resurrected on the third day. By accepting Jesus as my Lord and Savior, I believe You have forgiven all my sins and have now adopted me into Your family. Amen"

If you prayed that prayer, may I be the first to say, "WELCOME TO THE FAMILY OF GOD!!!" Your life here on earth and for all eternity has now greatly changed, and in the best way possible! Please tell someone about your decision to accept Jesus as your Lord and Savior and find a church family that you can join so they can help you navigate this beautiful life you have just chosen.

AND BEFORE WE CLOSE ...

I want to thank you for taking the time to read this book. I hope you will share it with others. My prayer is that throughout these pages, you have drawn closer to God as you have read and applied some of the important truths of our Christian faith. As you live a life serving God, know that He is patient and compassionate. He truly understands our struggles and is always ready to forgive us when we repent and turn away from sin and back to Him. Simply put... He is a good, good Father!

I pray that you will make spending time in God's Word and seeking Him a priority in your daily schedule. Know that God loves you unconditionally and has a great plan for your life, just as Jeremiah 29:11 tells us. May you find God in all the details of your life, both large and small. And may you recognize His presence with you every second of every day. Blessings to you!

Love and prayers, Linda

Printed in the USA
CPSIA information can be obtained
at www.ICGtesting.com
JSHW081141010923
47460JS00003B/13

9 781631 998775